THE WHOLE EARTH GEOGRAPHY BOOK

Anthony D. Fredericks

Illustrated by
Rebecca N. Fredericks

SCOTT, FORESMAN AND COMPANY

GLENVIEW, ILLINOIS   LONDON

To Dave Dunn
For early mornings filled with hot chocolate, good
conversation, and a puzzle or two!

Good Year Books
are available for preschool through Grade 12 and for every basic
curriculum subject plus many enrichment areas. For more Good Year
Books, contact your local bookseller or educational dealer. For a
complete catalog with information about other Good Year Books,
please write:

Good Year Books
Department GYB
1900 East Lake Avenue
Glenview, Illinois 60025

1991 Impression

ISBN 0-673-38639-2

6 PAT 94 93

Contents

Introduction

Since our earliest times, we human beings have been fascinated with our environment, excited by what might lie just over the horizon, and thrilled by the forms and functions of the planet we inhabit. Today we face a world that seems to be shrinking, because of advanced transportation and communication technology. So it is imperative that students understand and appreciate the interplay of human beings with locations, regions, countries, and continents both near and far. *The Whole Earth Geography Book* is designed to help students use their geography knowledge in real-life situations and explorations.

The Problem-Solving Approach

This book emphasizes problem-solving activities in which students can use higher-level thinking skills together with basic geographical facts. Students too often are given piles of factual data but little opportunity to think through various situations, formulate opinions, justify their responses, or interact with their classmates. The activities in this book challenge students by stimulating them to move beyond rote memorization of facts, into developing complex thought and making personal discoveries. Here is a sample problem:

> In a list of the five largest states, which of the following would not belong?
> salaka   anoiairflc   setax   rekwnoy

Several skills are necessary to solve this problem:

1. The student must rearrange the letters in each word in the proper sequence. (language arts, spelling) Note that, throughout the book, two-word names are treated as one name with no space between.

2. The student must obtain information on the relative sizes of various states. (atlas, encyclopedia)

3. The student must identify the five largest states and decide which of the states in the problem would not be included on that list. (problem solving, critical thinking)

This book presents a collection of activities, in a stimulating and fun format, that encourages students to actively process geographical knowledge. Intended for students in Grades 4 to 6, the book is also appropriate for gifted pupils in the lower grades.

Content Categories
The activities and information in this book are presented in three different categories — U.S. Geography, Map and Globe Skills, and World Geography:

1. U.S. Geography
The mountain ranges and rivers that crisscross our country, the states and their relationship to one another, and the influence of landforms on people and on what people do comprise this section of the book. Understanding the United States — its similarities and its divergence — make a fascinating subject for students to pursue. Appreciating the country they live in will be a valuable part of these activities for your students.

2. Map and Globe Skills
Meridians, time lines, boundaries, and poles are just a few of the topics covered in this section. Here students are provided with meaningful activities and real-life problems to solve as they discover more about the pictures, diagrams, and scales that represent the world we inhabit. Seeking answers to practical challenges gives students many experiences in discovering the functions and purposes of maps and globes.

3. World Geography
Hardly a day goes by that we are not reminded of events taking place in other parts of the world. Headlines from the Middle East, Asia, Central America, and Africa comprise a large portion of the news we get each day. Understanding where these countries are and how they relate to one another is a constant, exciting challenge. This section provides students with a host of possibilities for comprehending and appreciating world geography.

The data presented within these activities have been checked against many social studies texts normally used in the intermediate grades. So the data represent a cross section of information commonly given within each of the three major categories. Students thus have many opportunities to use prior knowledge with problem-solving skills to work out appropriate responses.

Daily Problems and Extended Challenges
The activities in this book are organized into two groups — Daily Problems and Extended Challenges.

Daily Problems
The book contains 192 Daily Problems — enough for every day of the school year. There are 64 problems in U.S. Geography, 64 in Map and Globe Skills, and 64 in World Geography. Initially,

you may wish to remove these pages from the book, paste them on oaktag, laminate them, and cut them apart into cards. Arrange the cards in a file box in sequential order or randomly. The problems can be used in one or more of the following ways:

1. When students arrive in the morning, or during a few moments a at the end of the day, ask them to each select a card at random and work on the listed problem. Personal charts can be initiated and individually maintained to record problems solved by each pupil.

2. Depending on the structure of your social studies text, you may wish to have students work in one subject area (U.S. Geography, Map and Globe Skills, or World Geography) until most of or all the problems in that section have been solved. Students may then move on to another section.

3. Post one card on the bulletin board for all students to solve during their free time.

4. Have students work in pairs, exchanging ideas and working together toward a mutual solution. This technique is particularly appropriate for below-level students.

5. Assign one card per day per student as a homework assignment.

Extended Challenges

The Extended Challenges require long-term investigations by students. These pages are designed to challenge students in assembling data, interpreting facts, organizing thoughts, and processing information. Students will need to use various types of reference materials, such as encyclopedias, globes, charts, and maps, to solve the problems successfully. You may wish to post an Extended Challenge on the bulletin board at the beginning of the week and provide multiple opportunities for students, either individually or in groups, to complete the page. These challenges can be used as homework assignments, too. However you plan to use these worksheets, it will be important for you to plan some time to discuss and share students' findings.

A word of caution is in order. Both Daily Problems and Extended Challenges are designed as *reinforcing* activities, and are not intended for the initial learning of geographical information. Both kinds of activities are most appropriate as a follow-up to the skills and concepts traditionally taught via your social studies text. All these activities can be used to strengthen and promote important ideas enumerated in the text. Thus they serve as a valuable adjunct to the entire social studies curriculum.

Although these activities are designed to enhance and extend your social studies curriculum, you should also encourage students to create similar problems and challenges for their classmates. This type of activity promotes the concept of active participation and stimulates a "hands-on" approach to the mastery of geographical concepts. Student involvement in designing other activities makes the study of geography exciting and dynamic. In turn, students are motivated to learn more about their country and their world.

These activities have been formulated for use in a variety of classrooms and a host of learning situations. You can use them as an adjunct to the social studies curriculum or as a reinforcement tool for vital concepts, and you are encouraged to use them in individual, small-group, or whole-class instructional situations. You are welcome to use the activities in whatever sequence you feel most appropriate. These problems and challenges offer you many opportunities to "energize" geography for your entire class.

Answers to both Daily Problems and Extended Challenges are presented at the end of the book. For some of the Extended Challenges, potential solutions are offered, because some answers depend on students' background and experience and on the changing nature of the world. When students' answers differ in some respect from those provided in the answer section, plan time to discuss students' rationale and reasoning. You may need to consult current maps and news sources to verify and/or confirm some responses. Helping students understand that geography is not a static subject is an important by-product of working with this book.

Daily Problems

★ U.S. Geography
Cards 1–64

★ U.S. Geography   1

Which of the following states does *not* touch California?

goneor   niaraoz   haut   deanav

★ U.S. Geography   2

If you were in New Orleans and were facing west, what body of water would be on your left side?

★ U.S. Geography   3

Fill in the puzzle with the names of states that border the Pacific Ocean.

★ U.S. Geography   4

In a list of the five largest states, which of the following would *not* belong?

salaka   anoiairflc   setax   rekwnoy

★ U.S. Geography   5

Which three states lie completely above 45°N?

★ U.S. Geography   6

If Cynthia drives from the capital of North Dakota direct to the capital of Washington, how many states will she pass through?

★ U.S. Geography   7

The fiftieth state has a characteristic shared by no other state. What is it?

★ U.S. Geography   8

Fill in the puzzle with the names of the capitals of southern states.

★ U.S. Geography   9

Fill in the puzzle with the names of states through which the Rocky Mountains run.

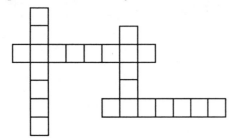

★ U.S. Geography   10

Which of the following states are in the Northeast?

netrovm   hodai   naemi   nakssa

★ U.S. Geography   11

Henry left Cheyenne, Wyoming, and traveled 200 miles due east. He then traveled 200 miles due south. What state was he in then?

★ U.S. Geography   12

The largest of the Great Lakes touches three states. What are the names of those states?

★ U.S. Geography   13

Which of the following is an abbreviation for a state located in the Southwest?

MN   PA   AZ   AL   NC

★ U.S. Geography   14

Fill in the puzzle with the names of states that have the Mississippi River as part of their borders.

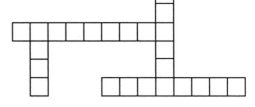

★ U.S. Geography   15

I am the state with the largest area and the smallest population. Who am I?

★ U.S. Geography   16

Glenda and her family are traveling through a New England state known for its potatoes. What state are they visiting?

From *The Whole Earth Geography Book*, Copyright © 1990 Scott, Foresman and Company.

★ **U.S. Geography**   17

I am the only state that does *not* have counties. Who am I?

★ **U.S. Geography**   18

Fill in the puzzle with the names of states through which the Continental Divide passes.

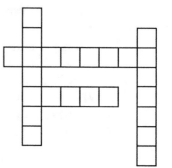

★ **U.S. Geography**   19

The only point in the United States where four states meet is known as

_____.

★ **U.S. Geography**   20

The Colorado River passes through me. The Grand Canyon is within my borders. Mexico is my southern neighbor. What state am I?

★ **U.S. Geography**   21

Carol traveled the length of the Rio Grande River. How many states does the river touch?

★ **U.S. Geography**   22

Fill in the puzzle with the names of states beginning with the letter *I*.

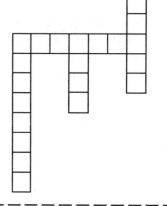

★ **U.S. Geography**   23

I am the only state split in two by a body of water. Who am I?

★ **U.S. Geography**   24

The Olympic Mountains, the Columbia River, and the Cascade Range are all part of my geography. What state am I?

Put a T in front of each true statement and an F in front of each false statement.

_____ Chicago is the state capital of Illinois.

_____ The Missouri River forms part of the border of Kansas.

_____ Mt. Whitney is the highest mountain in the United States.

_____ New Hampshire is next to a foreign country.

Taj lives in the largest city in northern California. His cousin Angela lives in a midwestern state, the capital of which is the last name of a U.S. president. If Taj flies directly to his cousin's home, which states will he pass over?

Which of the following deserts is in the United States?

Atacama
Mojave
Sahara
Gobi

Match the following by drawing lines from the items on the left to the corresponding items on the right.

state   Atlanta
city   Ohio
               New Jersey
               Helena
               Boston

Match the following by drawing lines from the items on the left to the corresponding items on the right.

Great Salt Lake   Arizona
Death Valley   California
Grand Canyon   Idaho
Snake River   Utah

I am the only national park in the state that has Santa Fe as its capital. Who am I?

Carrie lives in a state that has a foreign country, a famous river, and the most populous U.S. state as parts of its border. What is the capital of Carrie's state?

Which of the following is *not* a city in Georgia?

Athens
Miami
Atlanta
Columbus

From *The Whole Earth Geography Book*, Copyright © 1990 Scott, Foresman and Company.

★ U.S. Geography 33

The geographical center of the United States is located in which state?

★ U.S. Geography 34

The Mississippi River forms part of the border of which states?

★ U.S. Geography 35

Which of the following states has a desert?

CA   MN   FL   WA   PA

★ U.S. Geography 36

Match the following by drawing lines from the items on the left to their corresponding items on the right.

Northeast   Arkansas
Southeast   Vermont
Midwest   Oregon
West   Illinois

★ U.S. Geography 37

I am the lowest place in the United States. Which state is located directly east of me?

★ U.S. Geography 38

Which of the following states has the Atlantic Ocean as part of its border?

angiiirv   torvnme   nghiaicm   aaaambl

★ U.S. Geography 39

Which two states have four 90° corners?

★ U.S. Geography 40

Molly lives in a state that has a large river, a great lake, and the "Dairy State" as parts of its border. What is the largest city in Molly's state?

★ U.S. Geography   41

Which of the following states does *not* have
Canada as part of its border?

oaihd   aadinin   torvnme   aanmnto

★ U.S. Geography   42

Fill in the puzzle with the names
of the five
largest
states.

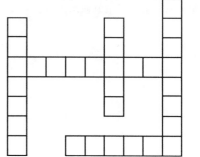

★ U.S. Geography   43

The Missouri River forms part of my boundary. The Mississippi River forms another
part of my boundary. South Dakota forms
another part of my boundary. What state
am I?

★ U.S. Geography   44

Which states have compass terms in their
names?

★ U.S. Geography   45

This state borders a foreign country, but
does *not* border another state. Which state
is it?

★ U.S. Geography   46

Which of the following states does *not* have
Oklahoma as part of its border?

sxtae   iusirosm   ssaank   giownmy

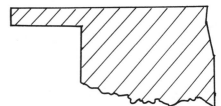

★ U.S. Geography   47

Hawaii is to island as Florida is to
_____.

North is to Carolina as *West* is to
_____.

Grand Canyon is to Arizona as Yellowstone
is to _____..

★ U.S. Geography   48

Tara lives in a state that has the same name
as the longest river in the United States.
What is the capital of the state directly to the
east of Tara's state?

From *The Whole Earth Geography Book,* Copyright © 1990 Scott, Foresman and Company.

★ U.S. Geography 49

Put a T in front of each true statement and an F in front of each false statement.

_____ Nome, Alaska, is further west than Honolulu, Hawaii
_____ Texas is larger than New York.
_____ The Mississippi River begins in Minnesota.
_____ Augusta is a state capital.

★ U.S. Geography 50

Which of the following states is *not* touched by one of the Great Lakes?

aadinin   nghimcia   ssakna   ohoi

★ U.S. Geography 51

Which of the following is (are) *not* true about Chicago?

A. It is further west than Kansas City.
B. It is located on one of the Great Lakes.
C. It is the capital of Illinois.
D. It is further north than Washington, DC.

★ U.S. Geography 52

Two state capitals are located on the Mississippi River. They are the capitals of which two states?

★ U.S. Geography 53

Nathan lives in a state that has four 90° corners, the Continental Divide, and the beginning of the Rio Grande River. What is the capital of that state?

★ U.S. Geography 54

Which states border the Gulf of Mexico?

★ U.S. Geography 55

Which of the following words is *not* used in the name of a state?

hrnot   uhtso   sate   ewts

★ U.S. Geography 56

Match the following by drawing lines from the items on the left to their corresponding items on the right.

state   Wisconsin
city   Harrisburg
               Kentucky
               Missouri
               Denver

Carson City is to Nevada as Memphis is to
_____.

Great Salt Lake is to Utah as Everglades is to
_____.

Golden is to California as *Keystone* is to
_____.

Fill in the puzzle with
the names of big rivers
of the United States.

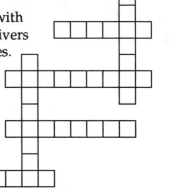

Pedro lives in a state whose borders include
a Great Lake, a midwestern state, a southern
state, and an eastern state. What is the
largest city in the state directly to the north
of Pedro's state?

Match the following by drawing lines from
the items on the left to their corresponding
items on the right.

shoreline   Arkansas
no shoreline   Texas
                     Virginia
                     South Carolina
                     Tennessee

Which of the following states is *not* in the
Rocky Mountain region?

dohai   oaooclrd   aanmotn   ssakna

The lowest point in the United States is 80
miles from the highest point in the continental United States. Which state are they both
in?

Which of these cities is in the Texas
Panhandle?

Amarillo
Forth Worth
El Paso
Corpus Christi

Match the following by drawing lines from
the items on the left to their corresponding
items on the right.

Pierre   N. Carolina
Columbia   N. Dakota
Bismarck   S. Carolina
Raleigh   S. Dakota

From *The Whole Earth Geography Book,* Copyright © 1990 Scott, Foresman and Company.

Daily Problems

■ Map and Globe Skills
Cards 65–128

■ Map & Globe Skills 65

If the scale on a map indicates that one inch equals 2 1/2 miles, how many miles would be indicated by eleven and one-half inches?

■ Map & Globe Skills 66

Which of the following indicate(s) longitude?

37°W   45°N   81°E   9°S

■ Map & Globe Skills 67

Write the abbreviations for each of the eight compass points; how many times did you use the letter *W*?

■ Map & Globe Skills 68

If you stood in Key West, Florida and faced east, what country would be to your right?

■ Map & Globe Skills 69

The Tropic of Capricorn passes through the countries named here, among others:

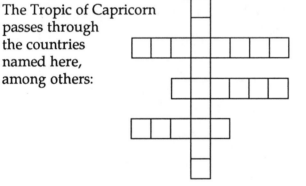

■ Map & Globe Skills 70

Harold sees this symbol on a map. What does it indicate?

■ Map & Globe Skills 71

How tall is a tree that is drawn to a scale of one inch to 32 feet if the height of the tree in the drawing is six and a quarter inches?

■ Map & Globe Skills 72

What is wrong with the following coordinates?

18°W/92°N

In which direction would you travel to go from Austin, Texas, to Little Rock, Arkansas?

The line of latitude numbered 0° is also known as _____.

What compass point is missing from the following list?

SW   N   SE   E   S   NW   W

If it is 8 A.M. in Boston, what time is it in Honolulu?

I am an imaginary line that passes through a town in England, one sea, and two continents. I am also known as 0° longitude. What's my other name?

Through which oceans does the Equator pass?

Which of the following cities is *not* a capital city located south of the Tropic of Cancer?

gakobkn   tarperai   toboag   henwidle

What direction would you take in traveling from the capital of Italy to the largest city in England?

■ Map & Globe Skills 81

What direction would you take to go from the capital of Norway to the capital of Switzerland?

■ Map & Globe Skills 82

I am the state closest to the Tropic of Cancer. Who am I?

■ Map & Globe Skills 83

Which of the following cities is the furthest west?

Los Angeles   Reno   San Diego   Las Vegas

■ Map & Globe Skills 84

The Arctic Circle is north of all the following latitudes *except* one. Which one?

65°   69°   59°   54°

■ Map & Globe Skills 85

Which of these pairs represents the longest distance?

Honolulu - San Francisco
San Francisco - New York
New York - London
London - Oslo

■ Map & Globe Skills 86

What does this symbol indicate on a map?

■ Map & Globe Skills 87

Which of the following is not a body of water?

lguf   msshitu   asirtt   enaoc

■ Map & Globe Skills 88

Which ocean is located south of 66½°S?

■ Map & Globe Skills   89

If it is 1 A.M. in Washington, D.C., what time is it in Honolulu, Hawaii?

■ Map & Globe Skills   90

What does the following symbol indicate on a map?

■ Map & Globe Skills   91

Match the following by drawing lines from terms on the left to the matching definitions on the right.

Meridian   line of latitude
Parallel   0° longitude
Equator   line of longitude
Prime Meridian   0° latitude

■ Map & Globe Skills   92

What continent is located in the Northern, Southern, *and* Western hemispheres?

■ Map & Globe Skills   93

On a map, which of the following represents a park?

A.   B.   C.   D.

■ Map & Globe Skills   94

Which of the following is closest to Lima, Peru?

Arctic Circle
Tropic of Cancer
Equator
Tropic of Capricorn

■ Map & Globe Skills   95

Which states are located north of 50°N latitude?

■ Map & Globe Skills   96

When it is 1 P.M. in the largest city in France, what time is it in the westernmost city in Peru?

From *The Whole Earth Geography Book*, Copyright © 1990 Scott, Foresman and Company.

■ Map & Globe Skills   97

Match the following by drawing lines from the items on the left to the corresponding items on the right.

hemisphere   Asia
continent   Atlantic
country   Kenya
ocean   western

■ Map & Globe Skills   98

If two cities are 1,250 miles apart, and the scale on a map is one inch = 500 miles, how far apart (in inches) would these cities be on the map?

■ Map & Globe Skills   99

Match the following by drawing lines from the items on the left to the corresponding items on the right.

latitude   Equator
longitude   Arctic Circle
                   Prime Meridian
                   International Date Line

■ Map & Globe Skills   100

Which of the following cities is the furthest east?

Miami, FL
Philadelphia, PA
Atlanta, GA
Washington, DC

■ Map & Globe Skills   101

In the following cross section, which landform is *not* represented?

valley
plateau
mountain
hills

■ Map & Globe Skills   102

Longitude is to north–south as
_____ is to east–west.
Mountain is to hill as
_____ is to sea.
North is to south as
_____ is to inland.

■ Map & Globe Skills   103

Which oceans are located in all four hemispheres?

■ Map & Globe Skills   104

The Tropic of Capricorn does *not* pass through which of the following countries?

eichl   aingaretn   lzrbai   yuuuagr

■ Map & Globe Skills   105

Longitude 120°W forms the boundary for two states. Which states are they?

■ Map & Globe Skills   106

Karen lives in Seattle, Washington, and wants to travel by plane to Miami, Florida, via New York and Atlanta. Which direction will the plane travel on the second leg of the trip?

■ Map & Globe Skills   107

Which of the following landforms has the lowest elevation?

teersd   lilh   nanomuti   ueapatl

■ Map & Globe Skills   108

Put a T in front of each true statement and an F in front of each false statement.

_____ Australia is both a country and a
        continent.
_____ The Equator runs east and west.
_____ South America is located completely
        within the Southern Hemisphere.
_____ The Arctic Circle passes through part
        of the United States.

■ Map & Globe Skills   109

When it is 3 P.M. in Oklahoma City, in how many minutes will it be 12 noon in Honolulu?

■ Map & Globe Skills   110

Which U.S. state has the 45° latitude line as a northern boundary?

■ Map & Globe Skills   111

Caribbean is to *Sea* as
Hudson is to _____.
Cape Horn is to South
America as Cape of Good
Hope is to _____.
Statute mile is to nautical
mile as land is to

_____.

■ Map & Globe Skills   112

Which of the following symbols indicates a state boundary?

A.   B.   C.

                        D.

From *The Whole Earth Geography Book*, Copyright © 1990 Scott, Foresman and Company.

■ Map & Globe Skills   113

Fill in the puzzle with the names of places through which the Prime Meridian passes.

■ Map & Globe Skills   114

NW is to *Northwest* as _____ is to *south-west*.
Southeast is to northwest as _____ is to northeast.
45° is to northwest as _____ is to west.

■ Map & Globe Skills   115

In what direction would you travel to go from the capital of Canada to the capital of the United States?

■ Map & Globe Skills   116

Which ocean is located completely within the Northern Hemisphere?

■ Map & Globe Skills   117

Which of the following is (are) false?

A. The North Pole is at 90° latitude.
B. The Tropic of Cancer is north of the Arctic Circle.
C. The Equator is a line of latitude.
D. The Prime Meridian is a line of latitude that passes through Greenwich, England.

■ Map & Globe Skills   118

Which countries would you fly over if you traveled by plane directly from Bombay to Tokyo?

■ Map & Globe Skills   119

What part of this drawing indicates a peninsula?

Grand Land

Big Ocean

■ Map & Globe Skills   120

How far is the largest city in Massachusetts from the state capital of Kansas?

■ Map & Globe Skills 121

Which of the following countries is not in the Eastern Hemisphere?

dagenln   adiin   arbmu   uerp

■ Map & Globe Skills 122

Match the following by drawing lines from the items on the left to the corresponding items on the right.

Tropic of Capricorn	23 1/2°S
Tropic of Cancer	66 1/2°N
Antarctic Circle	66 1/2°S
Arctic Circle	23 1/2°N

■ Map & Globe Skills 123

Put a T in front of each true statement and an F in front of each false statement.

_____ There are seven continents in the world.
_____ The Prime Meridian is a line of latitude.
_____ The Equator passes through the United States.
_____ The North Pole is at 100°N latitude.

■ Map & Globe Skills 124

When it is 9 A.M. in the capital of Brazil, what time is it in the capital of Australia?

■ Map & Globe Skills 125

The scale on a map is one centimeter = 320 km. How many *miles* apart are two cities if their map distance is nine centimeters?

■ Map & Globe Skills 126

Longitude is to latitude as meridian is to

_____.

Arctic is to Antarctic as north is to

_____.

75°E is to 105°W as 165°E is to

_____.

■ Map & Globe Skills 127

Which of the following longitudes does not pass through the Indian Ocean?

97°   51°   82°   19°   70°

■ Map & Globe Skills 128

Which oceans would you cross in sailing east from Buenos Aires to Perth?

Daily Problems

● World Geography
Cards 129–192

● **World Geography** 129

Fill in the puzzle with the names of countries in the Middle East.

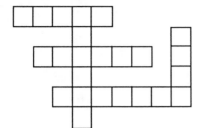

● **World Geography** 130

Jerry wishes to travel to an island nation that is part of Asia. Its capital has more people than any other country in Asia. What is the name of the country?

● **World Geography** 131

I am the largest inland sea on the Asian continent. Who am I?

● **World Geography** 132

Fill in the puzzle with the names of European countries that are on peninsulas.

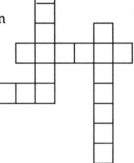

● **World Geography** 133

Maria wants to travel from the capital of Rumania to the largest city in Spain. What form of transportation would be the most direct?

atinr   nalep   cra   psih

● **World Geography** 134

I am a European country surrounded by water. I am close to the Arctic Circle. Who am I?

● **World Geography** 135

Indira sails east through the Strait of Gibraltar. What body of water is she entering?

● **World Geography** 136

Fill in the puzzle with the names of South American capital cities.

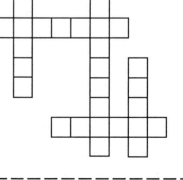

● World Geography   137

Which two seas form part of the border of Egypt?

● World Geography   138

Mongolia and India are countries on my border. I am famous for my Great Wall and the Yangtze River. Rice is a popular crop within my borders. Who am I?

● World Geography   139

Which of the following countries does *not* have Argentina as part of its border?

reup   liche   voiliab   guyruau

● World Geography   140

I am bordered by the Coral Sea and the Indian and Pacific oceans. New Zealand and Indonesia are my neighbors. Who am I?

● World Geography   141

What is the only Central American country whose name begins with a vowel?

● World Geography   142

What does this symbol indicate on a map?

● World Geography   143

Which two South American countries do *not* have an ocean as part of their border?

● World Geography   144

The largest river in the world has its mouth within my borders. Who am I?

● World Geography   145

Which of the following European countries does *not* border the Mediterranean Sea?

laiyt   cafner   naips   taisaur

● World Geography   146

Stand on me and everywhere you look is south. What am I?

● World Geography   147

Fill in the following puzzle with the names of Asian countries.

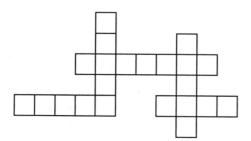

● World Geography   148

Which South American country has the driest desert in the world?

● World Geography   149

I am sometimes called the "Island Continent." Who am I?

● World Geography   150

Which of the following European countries have capital cities on the coast?

asnip   rutasai   noldap   dinlafn

● World Geography   151

Four continents begin with the letter *A* but only two are completely within the Southern Hemisphere.
Which two are they?

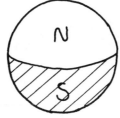

● World Geography   152

Which continent is bordered by the Pacific, Indian, and Arctic oceans?

● **World Geography**   153

Which of these countries is *not* an island?

aubc   npjaa   daeinlc   arkeo

● **World Geography**   154

Which of the following pairs have a sea
between the paired countries?

Egypt and Saudi Arabia
India and Burma
Sweden and Finland
Iraq and Syria

● **World Geography**   155

Match the following by drawing lines from
the terms on the left to the corresponding
terms on the right.

North America   Costa Rica
Central America   Colombia
South America   Canada

● **World Geography**   156

I am an island nation located in Asia. Manila
is my capital. Who am I?

● **World Geography**   157

Put a T in front of each true statement and
an F in front of each false statement.

_____ The USSR is the largest continent.
_____ Sofia is the capital of Rumania.
_____ Mongolia has no coastline.
_____ Libya is located on the African
        continent.

● **World Geography**   158

What is the only Great Lake named for a
Canadian province?

● **World Geography**   159

Fiji is located to the north of which country?

● **World Geography**   160

Which of the following rivers does *not* end
in the Atlantic Ocean?

Amazon
Mississippi
Niger
Loire

From *The Whole Earth Geography Book*, Copyright © 1990 Scott, Foresman and Company.

● World Geography 161

I am a country that extends almost a thousand miles from north to south. I consist of two main islands and several smaller ones. I am located in the Southern Hemisphere. Who am I?

● World Geography 162

Which of the following is the world's second largest country?

aihcn   aaandc   asrusi   lzriba

● World Geography 163

What is the capital city of the country that has the Great Victoria Desert, the Great Dividing Range, and the Great Barrier Reef?

● World Geography 164

Which of the following South American capital cities is furthest west?

Bogota
Sucre
Quito
Santiago

● World Geography 165

Which of the following capital cities is *not* in a European country?

nluibd   draidm   setanh   oiarc

● World Geography 166

On which continent would you find the Andes Mountains?

● World Geography 167

Match the following by drawing lines from the terms on the left to their corresponding terms on the right.

Madrid   Belgium
Brussels   Austria
Sofia   Bulgaria
Vienna   Spain

● World Geography 168

Clarence lives in a country that has the Atlantic Ocean, the Mediterranean Sea, and the Rhine River as portions of its borders. What country is located due east of the capital of Clarence's country?

● **World Geography**   **169**

Which of the following countries has the Atlantic Ocean as part of its border?

lgtoprua   njaap   muabr   arsaitu

● **World Geography**   **170**

I am the world's smallest country. I am also a city. Who am I?

● **World Geography**   **171**

Match the following by drawing a line from the items on the left to the corresponding items on the right.

Country   USSR
Continent   Asia
                 Antarctica
                 S. America
                 New Zealand

● **World Geography**   **172**

One South American country has two capitals. What are the names of those two cities?

● **World Geography**   **173**

Italy is to peninsula as Australia is to

_____.

Amazon is to *River* as *Mediterranean* is to

_____.

Alps are to mountains as Sahara is to

_____.

● **World Geography**   **174**

Which of the following countries is *not* a neighbor of Australia?

New Zealand
Indonesia
New Guinea
Korea

● **World Geography**   **175**

Which two oceans does the Panama Canal connect?

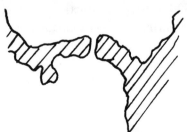

● **World Geography**   **176**

I am the smallest continent in the world. I am the only continent that is a single country. I am sometimes referred to as "The Land Down Under." Who am I?

From *The Whole Earth Geography Book,* Copyright © 1990 Scott, Foresman and Company.

● **World Geography** 177

The Nile River flows through all the following countries except one. Which one?

angdua　　tepgy　　nsaud　　aziabm

● **World Geography** 178

The largest inland sea is located in which country?

● **World Geography** 179

Which of the following countries is the largest (in square miles)?

India
Brazil
China
Australia

● **World Geography** 180

Marta lives in a country bordered by the Black Sea, the Danube River, and a country whose capital is Belgrade. What is the capital of the country to the north of Marta's country?

● **World Geography** 181

Put a T in fron of each true statement and an F in front of each false statement.

_____ Belize is a Central American country.
_____ Sri Lanka is an island nation.
_____ Japan's nearest neighbor is China.
_____ The Falkland Islands lie off the coat of Argentina.

● **World Geography** 182

What is the capital of the country in which Mt. Everest is located?

● **World Geography** 183

Which of the following cities is *not* located in Central America?

Managua
Caracas
San Jose
San Salvador

● **World Geography** 184

Match the following by drawing lines from the terms on the left to their corresponding terms on the right.

sea　　　　Persian
ocean　　　Mediterranean
bay　　　　Indian
gulf　　　　Hudson

The largest country in South America borders which ocean?

Which of the following cities is *not* located on the west coast of its respective country?

Vancouver
Perth
Rome
Buenos Aires

Fill in the puzzle with the names of Central American countries. Treat two-part names as one word, with no space between.

Which of the following South American countries does *not* have Bolivia as part of its border?

uepr   lzrbia   auuuryg   ecihl

Match the following items by drawing a line from the items on the left to the corresponding items on the right.

country   Panama
continent   Australia
                 India
                 Europe
                 Africa

Julio's father works in a country bordered by the Arabian Sea and the Bay of Bengal. What is the capital of the country on the northwestern border of the country where Julio's father works?

Marie Byrd Land, Mt. Markham, and the Ross Ice Shelf can be found on which continent?

I am the largest country on the world's largest continent. Who am I?

From *The Whole Earth Geography Book*, Copyright © 1990 Scott, Foresman and Company.

Extended Challenges

Worksheets 1–15

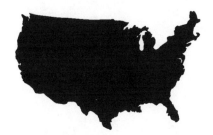

Identify the <u>capital</u> for each of the following states.

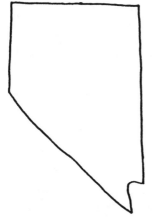

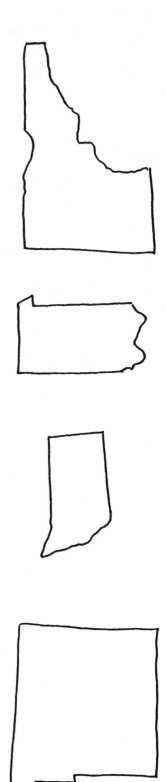

Identify an example of each landform, and place each one on the proper continent. One sample has been done for you.

Landform	Example	Continent
lake	Sahara	Australia
desert	Hudson	South America
peninsula	Alps	Antarctica
island	Eyre	Asia
bay	Amazon	North America
mountains	Palmer	Africa
river	Japan	Europe

(island — Japan — Asia)

Extended Challenge 3

Name _____

Date _____

Place a check mark after each country to show which
hemisphere(s) it is in.

Hemispheres

	Eastern	Western	Northern	Southern
Turkey	✓		✓	
India				
Antarctica				
Uruguay				
Greenland				
Australia				
Mexico				
South Africa				
Japan				
Thailand				
Canada				
Bolivia				
New Zealand				
Chile				
Venezuela				

Name _____

Date _____

In the puzzle below, locate and circle the names of all the states that have a seacoast. The names will go down, across, or diagonally. One state with a seacoast is missing from the puzzle. Write its name on the line under the puzzle. Two-part names are spelled as one, with no space between parts.

```
R  L  C  M  I  S  S  I  S  S  I  P  P  I  H  T  G
N  Q  O  I  I  G  I  H  J  M  N  B  K  N  O  N  M
O  N  H  M  A  I  N  Z  W  A  V  R  M  Y  O  G  W
R  K  A  L  A  S  K  A  H  R  O  S  N  G  N  X  A
T  C  P  W  F  I  J  F  L  Y  U  S  E  X  E  O  S
H  G  A  E  J  G  N  K  W  L  L  R  W  E  W  R  H
C  H  D  L  V  D  E  E  N  A  O  C  H  F  J  H  I
A  J  E  O  I  I  N  O  X  N  U  R  A  M  E  O  N
R  S  L  R  R  F  W  Q  R  D  I  P  M  T  R  D  G
O  S  A  Z  G  L  O  Z  A  G  S  B  P  M  S  E  T
L  J  W  A  I  O  Q  R  W  T  I  H  S  L  E  I  O
I  Y  A  V  N  R  U  V  N  K  A  A  H  C  Y  S  N
N  K  R  X  I  I  D  W  P  I  N  E  I  E  A  L  G
A  T  E  P  A  D  D  B  B  K  A  E  R  X  D  A  V
D  Y  U  Y  I  A  L  A  B  A  M  A  E  F  U  N  R
Q  C  O  N  N  E  C  T  I  C  U  T  B  L  F  D  C
Z  A  C  A  S  O  U  T  H  C  A  R  O  L  I  N  A
```

The state with a seacoast not included in the puzzle above: _____

On the illustration below, label the following:

island	peninsula	tributary	delta	channel
inlet	sound	strait	bay	gulf
sea	river	lake	cape	canal

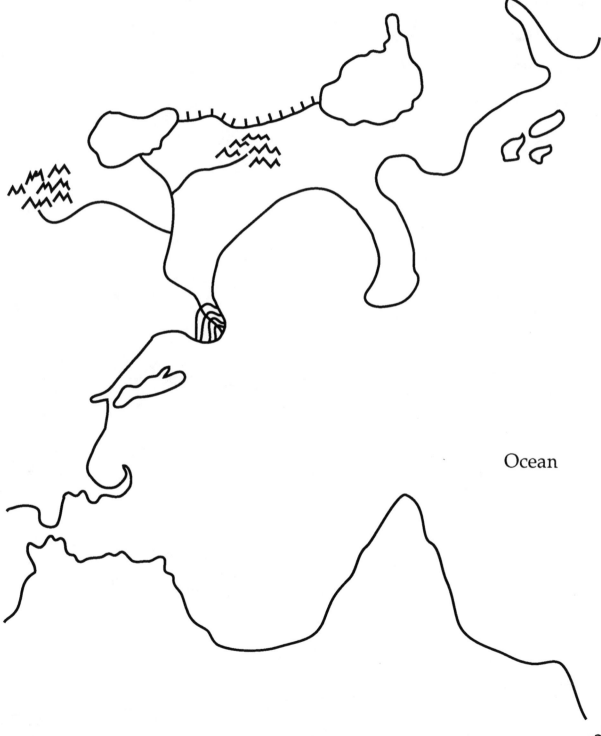

Ocean

Extended Challenge 6

Put a letter from the column on the left in front of each city in the right column to indicate which of the east-west lines it is closest to.

A. Arctic Circle

B. Tropic of Cancer

C. Equator

D. Tropic of Capricorn

E. Antarctic Circle

_____ Addis Ababa

_____ Kampala

_____ Oslo

_____ Cairo

_____ Rio de Janeiro

_____ Singapore

_____ Tokyo

_____ Rangoon

_____ Brisbane

_____ Nome

_____ Taipei

_____ Tripoli

_____ Riyadh

_____ Helsinki

_____ Quito

_____ Reykjavik

_____ Pretoria

_____ Bogota

_____ Nassau

_____ Calcutta

Some of the following statements are true about South America, others are false. Identify those that are false, and rewrite them to make them correct.

_____ 1. Bolivia, Paraguay, and Uruguay are the only inland countries.

_____ 2. The Equator passes through three countries.

_____ 3. The capital of Brazil is located on the Atlantic Ocean.

_____ 4. From north to south, Chile is the longest country.

_____ 5. The country closest to the Panama Canal is Colombia.

_____ 6. The Amazon River begins in the Andes Mountains.

_____ 7. The South American continent is bordered by an ocean and a sea.

_____ 8. South America extends below the Tropic of Capricorn.

_____ 9. Guyana is the smallest country.

_____ 10. The Falkland Islands lie off the coast of Argentina.

_____ 11. Much of Peru lies in the Andes Mountains.

_____ 12. Suriname is located west of Venezuela.

_____ 13. Montevideo is an Atlantic coast country.

_____ 14. Argentina is split into two parts.

_____ 15. Colombia, Brazil, and Peru each forms part of the border of Equador.

Name

Date

Draw a line from each of the states in the middle column to its capital in the left column, and then to its corresponding region in the right column. One sample has been done for you.

Capital	State	Region
Cheyenne	New Mexico	Northeast
Concord	West Virginia	Southeast
Juneau	Ohio	Midwest
Columbus	North Dakota	Mountain
Charleston	Montana	Pacific
Jackson	Mississippi	
Bismarck	Wisconsin	
Albany	Wyoming	
Little Rock	Oregon	
Santa Fe	Alaska	
Helena	New Hampshire	
Madison	New York	
Olympia	Arkansas	
Salem	Washington	

Name

Date

Complete the puzzle below by filling in the spaces with the names of lines, areas, or locations types of lines you would find on a map of the world. Treat multiple-word terms as one word, with no space between.

```
                        L _ _ G _ _ _ _ _
                        _ _ I _
    _ _ _ P _ _ _ _ _ _ _ N _ _ _
        _ _ _ _ _ _ _ E _ _ _ _ _ _
                        S _ _ _ H _ _ _ _
            _ Q _ _ _ O _
        _ _ _ _ _ _ _ N _
            _ _ _ T _ C _ _ _ _ _ _
        _ _ _ _ _ _ _ H _ _ _
    _ _ T _ _ _ _ E
                        M _ _ _ _ _ _ _
        _ _ _ A _ _ _ _ _ _ _ _ _ _ _
                        P _ _ _ L _ _ _
```

Extended Challenge 10

The puzzle below contains the names of 32 European
countries. The names go across, down, or diagonally. Circle
each one in the puzzle. Two-word names are treated as one
word, with no space between.

```
L  C  D  H  Q  A  E  A  S  T  G  E  R  M  A  N  Y  U
I  O  S  A  N  M  A  R  I  N  O  P  H  P  B  A  P  N
E  V  A  T  I  C  A  N  C  I  T  Y  P  E  U  N  C  I
C  U  N  E  T  H  E  R  L  A  N  D  S  A  L  D  O  T
H  C  F  K  B  C  Z  A  M  Q  Z  G  O  M  G  O  H  E
T  B  Z  F  E  C  N  O  O  H  U  N  G  A  R  Y  D
E  E  M  E  R  U  Y  W  N  C  N  R  W  G  R  R  L  K
N  L  R  V  C  A  U  S  T  R  I  A  U  B  I  A  U  I
S  G  D  F  T  H  G  F  Z  T  V  B  C  I  A  V  X  N
T  I  E  I  S  P  O  L  A  N  D  J  J  O  J  F  E  G
E  U  N  N  Y  A  S  S  Y  M  S  M  D  Y  L  D  M  D
I  M  M  L  T  L  L  N  L  E  X  A  S  C  E  N  B  O
N  I  A  A  X  B  A  P  X  O  J  L  X  W  Q  I  O  M
L  T  R  N  D  A  V  Y  O  D  V  T  S  Z  M  D  U  B
I  K  K  D  S  N  I  R  M  R  K  A  E  W  N  A  R  X
R  U  M  A  N  I  A  J  X  R  T  L  K  A  M  G  G  I
E  T  U  D  I  A  S  R  A  E  W  U  L  I  K  N  G  L
L  H  L  C  S  G  Q  P  W  V  F  E  G  G  A  Q  A  H
A  J  E  B  Y  F  F  R  A  N  C  E  T  A  O  Y  H  V
N  O  R  W  A  Y  Z  S  W  I  T  Z  E  R  L  A  N  D
D  W  E  S  T  G  E  R  M  A  N  Y  K  U  P  B  I  D
```

From *The Whole Earth Geography Book*, Copyright © 1990 Scott, Foresman and Company.

Match each river in the left column with the names of the
states in the right column that have that river as part of
their border.

A. Colorado River

B. Ohio River

C. Missouri River

D. Columbia River

E. Red River

F. Delaware River

_____ Indiana

_____ Nebraska

_____ California

_____ Oklahoma

_____ Iowa

_____ Ohio

_____ Washington

_____ Pennsylvania

_____ South Dakota

_____ West Virginia

_____ Kansas

_____ Nevada

_____ Arkansas

_____ New Jersey

_____ Oregon

_____ Texas

_____ Illinois

_____ New York

_____ Arizona

_____ Kentucky

Name _____

Date _____

Draw a line from each capital city (left column) to its country (middle column) and then to that country's continent (right column). One sample has been done for you.

Capital	Country	Continent
Ottawa	China	North America
Stockholm	Canada	Africa
Caracas	Egypt	Asia
Beijing	Italy	Antarctica
Cairo	Sweden	South America
Rome	Portugal	Australia
Lagos	Australia	Europe
Ankara	Finland	
Helsinki	Turkey	
Quito	Venezuela	
Riyadh	Nigeria	
Lisbon	Congo	
Dakar	Senegal	
Canberra	Equador	
Brazzaville	Saudi Arabia	

44

Extended Challenge 13

Write the state's name in the blank after the clue or description.

1. Mississippi, Georgia, and Alabama are its southern neighbors. _____

2. OK is its state abbreviation. _____

3. The lowest point in the United States is here. _____

4. This state's capital is the same as the name of the sixteenth president. _____

5. This state is mainly a peninsula. _____

6. The Grand Canyon is located here. _____

7. This state has the largest body of salt water within its borders. _____

8. Frankfort is this state's capital. _____

9. The beginning of the Mississippi River starts here. _____

10. This is the smallest state. _____

11. Ohio is the eastern neighbor of this state. _____

12. Four Great Lakes touch this state. _____

13. This state is completely surrounded by water. _____

14. Washington is the northern neighbor of this state. _____

15. The Brooks Range is in this state. _____

In the blank, write the name of the country you would be in if you stood at each of the following coordinates.

1. 45°N/0°long _____

2. 30°S/31°E _____

3. 30°S/150°E _____

4. 40°N/4°W _____

5. 45°N/76°W _____

6. 60°N/75°E _____

7. 36°N/140°E _____

8. 30°S/60°W _____

9. 15°N/121°E _____

10. 45°N/105°E _____

11. 21°N/158°W _____

12. 15°S/75°W _____

13. 52°N/0°long _____

14. 30°N/30°E _____

15. 33°S/71°W _____

From *The Whole Earth Geography Book*, Copyright © 1990 Scott, Foresman and Company.

Complete the puzzle below by filling in the spaces with the names of capitals of Asian countries.

```
        _ A _ _ _ _ _
          S _ _ _ _
        _ _ I _ _ _
          _ A _ _ _ _ _
        _ _ N _ _ _ _
        _ _ C _ _
        _ _ A _  _ _ _ _ _
      _ _ _ _ _ P _ _ _
    _ _ _  _ _ _ _ I
          T _ _ _ _
        _ A _ _ _ _
        _ _ L _ _ _ _
        _ S _ _ _ _ _ _ _
```

Answer Key

Daily Problems
Extended Challenges

1. Oregon, Arizona, <u>Utah</u>, Nevada
2. Gulf of Mexico
3.

```
                W
                A                 H
                S                 A
                H         O       W
  C A L I F O R N I A
                L         N       I
                A         G       I
                S         T
                K         O
                A         N
```

4. Alaska, California, Texas, <u>New York</u>
5. Washington, North Dakota, Alaska
6. North Dakota, Montana, Idaho, Washington
7. It's completely surrounded by water; it's an island.
8.

```
                    R A L E I G H
        J                 T
N A S H V I L L E
        C                 A
        K                 N
        S                 T
C O L U M B I A
        N
```

9.

```
        W
        Y                 I
C O L O R A D O
        M                 A
        I                 H
        N         M O N T A N A
        G
```

10. <u>Vermont</u>, Idaho, <u>Maine</u>, Kansas
11. Kansas
12. Minnesota, Wisconsin, Michigan
13. AZ
14.

```
                          A
                          R
                          K
                          A
                          N
W I S C O N S I N
        O                 S
        W                 A
        A         M I S S O U R I
```

15. Alaska
16. Maine
17. Louisiana

50

From *The Whole Earth Geography Book*, Copyright © 1990 Scott, Foresman and Company.

18.

```
W                 M
Y                 O
C O L O R A D O   N
M                 T
I D A H O         A
N                 N
G                 A
                  A
```

19. Four Corners
20. Arizona
21. Colorado, New Mexico, Texas
22.

```
                I
                D
I N D I A N A   A
L       O       H
L       W       O
I       A
N
O
I
S
```

23. Michigan
24. Washington
25. F, T, F, T
26. California, Nevada, Utah, Colorado, Nebraska
27. Mojave
28. States — Ohio, New Jersey; Cities — Atlanta, Helena, Boston
29. Great Salt Lake — Utah; Death Valley — California; Grand Canyon— Arizona; Snake River — Idaho
30. Carlsbad Caverns National Park
31. Phoenix
32. Miami
33. South Dakota
34. Minnesota, Wisconsin, Iowa, Illinois, Missouri, Kentucky, Tennessee, Arkansas, Mississippi, Louisiana
35. CA
36. Northeast — Vermont; Southeast — Arkansas; Midwest — Illinois; West — Oregon
37. Nevada
38. <u>Virginia</u>, Vermont, Michigan, Alabama
39. Colorado, Wyoming
40. Chicago
41. Idaho, <u>Indiana</u>, Vermont, Montana

42.

```
                C
                A
                L
                I
M       T       F
O       E       O
N E W M E X I C O
T       A       R
A       S       N
A               I
     A L A S K A
```

43. Iowa
44. South Dakota, North Dakota, North Carolina, South Carolina, West Virginia
45. Alaska
46. Texas, Missouri, Kansas, <u>Wyoming</u>
47. Peninsula, *Virginia*, Wyoming
48. Montgomery
49. T, T, T, T
50. Indiana, Michigan, <u>Kansas</u>, Ohio
51. A, C
52. Minnesota, Louisiana
53. Denver
54. Texas, Louisiana, Mississippi, Alabama, Florida
55. North, South, <u>East</u>, West
56. States — Wisconsin, Kentucky, Missouri; Cities — Harrisburg, Denver
57. Tennessee, Florida, Pennsylvania
58.

```
                C
                O
                L
      H U D S O N
                R
                A
  M             D
  R I O G R A N D E
  S             O
  S
C O L U M B I A
  U
  R
O H I O
```

59. New York City
60. Shoreline — Texas, Virginia, South Carolina; no shoreline — Arkansas, Tennessee
61. Idaho, Colorado, Montana, <u>Kansas</u>
62. California
63. Amarillo
64. Pierre — S. Dakota; Columbia — S. Carolina; Bismark — N. Dakota; Raleigh — N. Carolina
65. 28¾ miles
66. 37°W, 81°E

From *The Whole Earth Geography Book*, Copyright © 1990 Scott, Foresman and Company.

67. Three
68. Cuba
69.

```
            A
            U
  B O T S W A N A
            T
      B R A Z I L
            A
  C H I L E
            I
            A
```

70. Hospital
71. 200 feet
72. Latitude, not longitude, should be listed first
73. Northeast
74. The Equator
75. NE
76. 3 A.M.
77. Prime Meridian
78. Pacific, Atlantic, Indian
79. Bangkok, Pretoria, Bogota, <u>New Delhi</u>
80. Northwest
81. South-southwest
82. Florida
83. Reno
84. 69°
85. New York–London
86. Canal
87. Gulf, <u>isthmus</u>, strait, ocean
88. Antarctic Ocean
89. 8 P.M.
90. Interstate Highway
91. Meridian — Line of longitude; Parallel — Line of latitude; Equator — 0° latitude; Prime Meridian — 0° longitude
92. South America
93. B.
94. Equator
95. Alaska
96. 7 A.M.
97. Hemisphere — Western; continent — Asia; country — Kenya; ocean — Atlantic
98. 2½ inches
99. Latitude — Equator, Arctic Circle; longitude — Prime Meridian, International Date Line
100. Philadelphia, PA
101. Plateau
102. Latitude, ocean, offshore
103. Pacific, Atlantic
104. Chile, Argentina, Brazil, <u>Uruguay</u>
105. California, Nevada
106. South-southwest
107. <u>Desert</u>, hill, mountain, plateau
108. T, T, F, T
109. Sixty minutes

110. Wyoming
111. *Bay*, Africa, sea
112. B.
113.

```
            A       S
            L       P
      F     G       A
    G R E E N W I C H
      A     R       N
      N     I
      C   A T L A N T I C
      E
```

114. SW, southwest, 90°
115. South
116. Arctic
117. B, D
118. India, Bangladesh, Burma, China, Japan
119.

120. 1350 miles (approximately)
121. England, India, Burma, <u>Peru</u>
122. Tropic of Capricorn — 23½°S; Tropic of Cancer —
    23½°N; Antarctic Circle — 66½°S; Arctic Circle — 66½°N
123. T, F, F, F
124. 10 P.M.
125. 1788 miles
126. Parallel, south, 15°W
127. 19°
128. Atlantic, Indian
129.

```
    S Y R I A
        S           I
    J O R D A N     R
        A           A
      L E B A N O N
        L
```

130. Japan

131.

```
              N
              O
              R       D
            S W E D E N
              A       N
        I T A L Y      M
                       A
                       R
                       K
```

132. Caspian Sea
133. Train, <u>plane</u>, car, ship
134. Iceland
135. Mediterranean Sea

136.

```
          L       S
        C A R A C A S
          P       N
          A       T     Q
          Z       I     U
                  A     I
            B O G O T A
                  O     O
```

137. Mediterranean, Red
138. China
139. <u>Peru</u>, Chile, Bolivia, Uruguay
140. Australia
141. El Salvador
142. National capital city
143. Bolivia, Paraguay
144. Brazil
145. Italy, France, Spain, <u>Austria</u>
146. North Pole

147.

```
              C
              H         J
          V I E T N A M
              N         P
        B U R M A   L A O S
                        N
```

148. Chile
149. Australia
150. Spain, Austria, Poland, <u>Finland</u>
151. Australia, Antarctica
152. Asia
153. Cuba, Japan, Iceland, <u>Korea</u>
154. Egypt and Saudi Arabia
155. North America — Canada; Central America — Costa Rica; South America — Columbia
156. Philippines
157. F, F, T, T
158. Lake Ontario
159. New Zealand
160. Mississippi

161. New Zealand
162. China, <u>Canada</u>, Russia, Brazil
163. Canberra
164. Quito
165. Dublin, Madrid, Athens, <u>Cairo</u>
166. South America
167. Madrid — Spain; Brussels — Belgium; Sofia — Bulgaria; Vienna — Austria
168. West Germany
169. <u>Portugal</u>, Japan, Burma, Austria
170. Vatican City
171. Countries — USSR, New Zealand; continents — Asia, Antarctica, South America
172. La Paz, Sucre
173. Continent, *sea*, desert
174. Korea
175. Atlantic and Pacific
176. Australia
177. Uganda, Egypt, Sudan, <u>Zambia</u>
178. USSR
179. China
180. Bucharest
181. T, T, F, T
182. Kathmandu
183. Caracas
184. Sea — Mediterranean; ocean — Indian; bay — Hudson; gulf — Persian
185. Atlantic
186. Buenos Aires
187.

```
          N I C A R A G U A
                        U
                        A
          H             T
          O             E
          N             M
          D   B         A   P
          U   E L S A L V A D O R
          R   L         A   N
  C O S T A R I C A         A
          S   Z             M
          E                 A
```

188. Peru, Brazil, <u>Uruguay</u>, Chile
189. Countries — Panama, Australia, India; continents — Australia, Europe, Africa
190. Islamabad
191. Antarctica
192. USSR

Extended Challenge 1

Identify the capital for each of the following states.

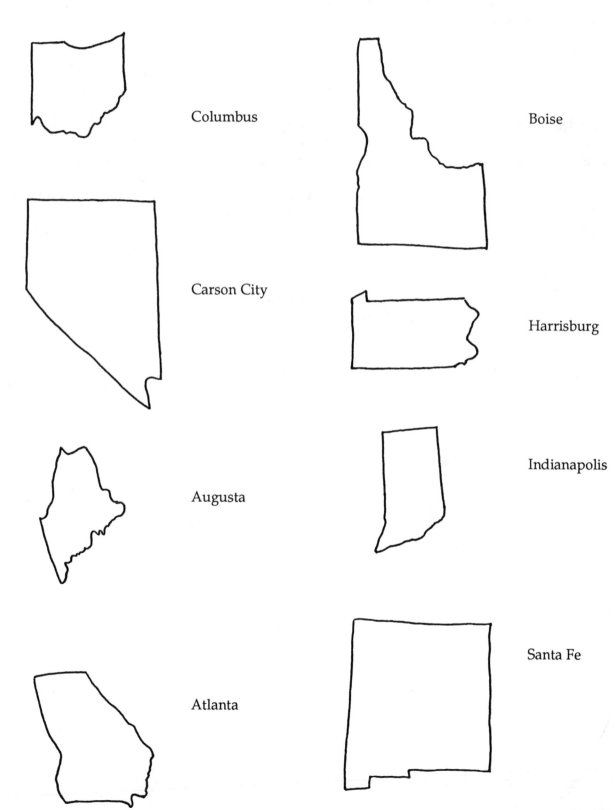

Columbus

Boise

Carson City

Harrisburg

Augusta

Indianapolis

Santa Fe

Atlanta

Extended Challenge 2

Identify an example of each landform, and place
each one on the proper continent. One sample has
been done for you.

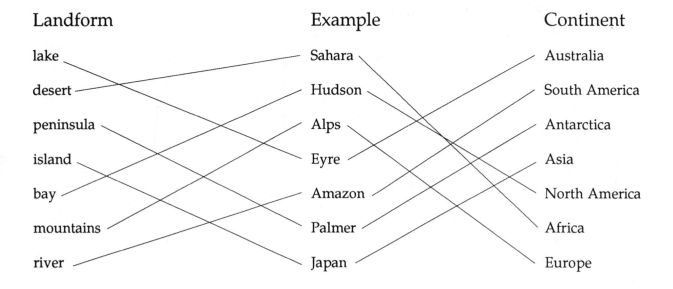

Landform	Example	Continent
lake	Sahara	Australia
desert	Hudson	South America
peninsula	Alps	Antarctica
island	Eyre	Asia
bay	Amazon	North America
mountains	Palmer	Africa
river	Japan	Europe

Extended Challenge 3

Place a check mark after each country to show which hemisphere(s) it is in.

Hemispheres

	Eastern	Western	Northern	Southern
Turkey	✔		✔	
India	✔		✔	
Antarctica	✔	✔		✔
Uruguay		✔		✔
Greenland		✔	✔	
Australia	✔			✔
Mexico		✔	✔	
South Africa	✔			✔
Japan	✔		✔	
Thailand	✔		✔	
Canada		✔	✔	
Bolivia		✔		✔
New Zealand	✔			✔
Chile		✔		✔
Venezuela		✔		✔

Extended Challenge 4

In the puzzle below, locate and circle the names of all the
states that have a seacoast. The names will go down,
across, or diagonally. One state with a seacoast is missing
from the puzzle. Write its name on the line under the
puzzle. Two-part names are spelled as one, with no space
between parts.

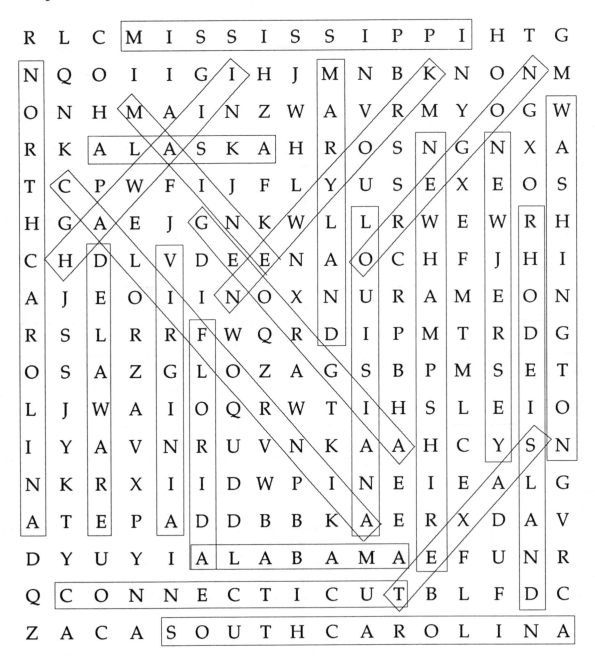

The state with a seacoast not included in the puzzle above: _____ Massachusetts _____

From *The Whole Earth Geography Book*, Copyright © 1990 Scott, Foresman and Company.

Extended Challenge 5

On the illustration below, label the following:

island   peninsula   tributary   delta   channel
inlet   sound   strait   bay   gulf
sea   river   lake   cape   canal

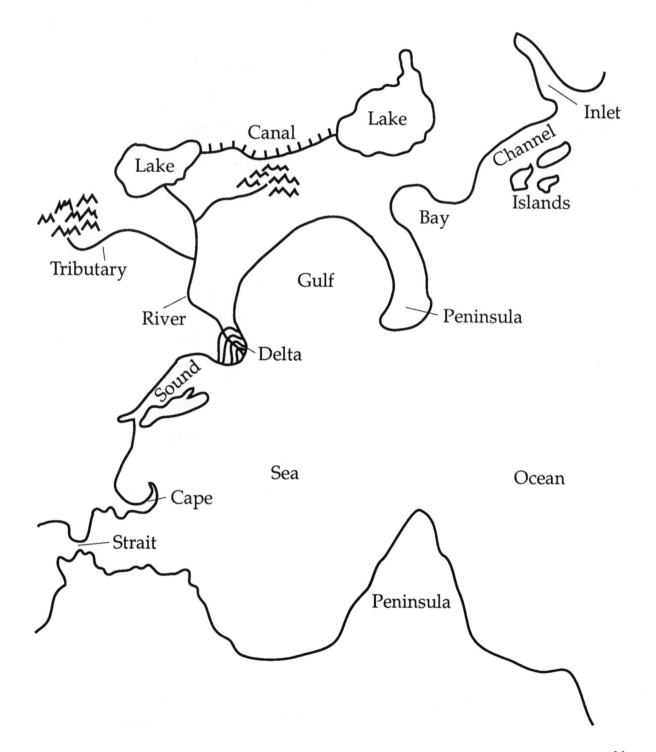

Extended Challenge 6

Put a letter from the column on the left in front of each city
in the right column to indicate which of the east-west lines
it is closest to.

A. Arctic Circle

B. Tropic of Cancer

C. Equator

D. Tropic of Capricorn

E. Antarctic Circle

__C__ Addis Ababa

__C__ Kampala

__A__ Oslo

__B__ Cairo

__D__ Rio de Janeiro

__C__ Singapore

__B__ Tokyo

__B__ Rangoon

__D__ Brisbane

__A__ Nome

__B__ Taipei

__B__ Tripoli

__B__ Riyadh

__A__ Helsinki

__C__ Quito

__A__ Reykjavik

__D__ Pretoria

__C__ Bogota

__B__ Nassau

__B__ Calcutta

From *The Whole Earth Geography Book*, Copyright © 1990 Scott, Foresman and Company.

Extended Challenge 7

Some of the following statements are true about South America, others are false. Identify those that are false, and rewrite them to make them correct.

__F__ 1. Bolivia, Paraguay, ~~and Uruguay~~ are the only inland countries.

__T__ 2. The Equator passes through three countries.

__F__ 3. The capital of Brazil is located ~~on~~ the ~~Atlantic Ocean~~.
                              in   interior.

__F__ 4. From north to south, ~~Chile~~ is the longest country.
                    Brazil

__T__ 5. The country closest to the Panama Canal is Colombia.

__T__ 6. The Amazon River begins in the Andes Mountains.

__F__ 7. The South American continent is bordered by ~~an ocean~~ and a sea.
                            two oceans

__T__ 8. South America extends below the Tropic of Capricorn.

__F__ 9. ~~Guyana~~ is the smallest country.
       French Guiana

__T__ 10. The Falkland Islands lie off the coast of Argentina.

__T__ 11. Much of Peru lies in the Andes Mountains.

__F__ 12. Suriname is located ~~west~~ of Venezuela.
              east

__F__ 13. Montevideo is an Atlantic coast ~~country~~.
                city

__T__ 14. Argentina is split into two parts.

__F__ 15. Colombia, ~~Brazil~~, and Peru each form part of the border of Equador.

Extended Challenge 8

Draw a line from each of the states in the middle column to its capital in the left column, and then to its corresponding region in the right column. One sample has been done for you.

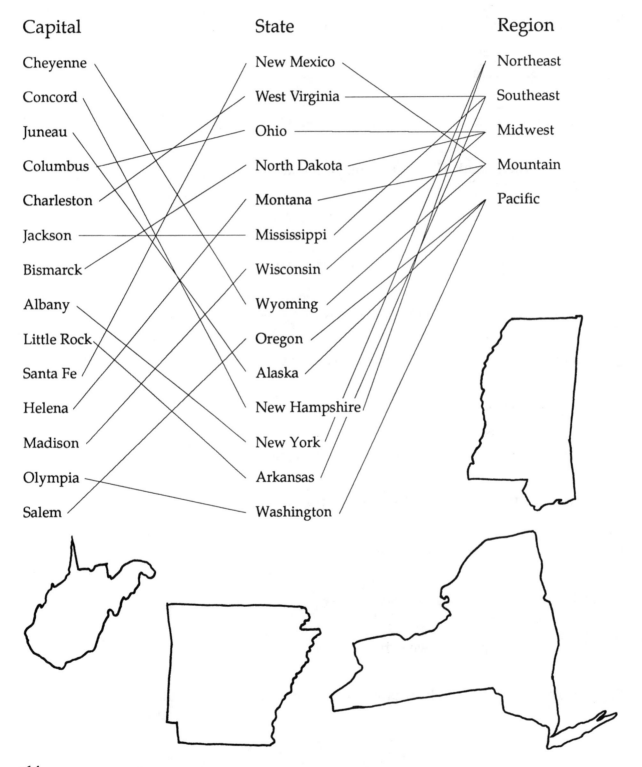

Capital	State	Region
Cheyenne	New Mexico	Northeast
Concord	West Virginia	Southeast
Juneau	Ohio	Midwest
Columbus	North Dakota	Mountain
Charleston	Montana	Pacific
Jackson	Mississippi	
Bismarck	Wisconsin	
Albany	Wyoming	
Little Rock	Oregon	
Santa Fe	Alaska	
Helena	New Hampshire	
Madison	New York	
Olympia	Arkansas	
Salem	Washington	

From *The Whole Earth Geography Book*, Copyright © 1990 Scott, Foresman and Company.

Complete the puzzle below by filling in the spaces with the names of lines, areas, or locations you would find on a map of the world. Treat multiple-word terms as one word, with no space between.

```
                    L O N G I T U D E
                 G R I D
     T R O P I C O F C A N C E R
           P R I M E M E R I D I A N
                    S O U T H P O L E
           E Q U A T O R
           D A T E L I N E
                A R C T I C C I R C L E
           H E M I S P H E R E
        L A T I T U D E
                    M E R I D I A N
           A N T A R C T I C C I R C L E
              P A R A L L E L
```

Extended Challenge 10

The puzzle below contains the names of 32 European
countries. The names go across, down, or diagonally. Circle
each one in the puzzle. Two-word names are treated as one
word, with no space between.

```
L   C D H Q A E A S T G E R M A N Y   U
I   O S A N M A R I N O P H P B A P   N
E   V A T I C A N C I T Y P E U D O   I
C   U N E T H E R L A N D S A L D H   T
H   C F K B C Z A M Q Z G O M G O H   E
T   B Z F E C E N O O H U N G A R Y   D
E   E M E R U Y W N C N R W G R R L   K
N   L R V C A U S T R I A U B I A U   I
S   G D F T H G F Z T V B C I A V X   N
T   I E I S P O L A N D J J O J F E   G
E   U N N Y A S S Y M S M D Y L D M   D
I   M M L T L L N L E X A S C E N B   O
N   I A A X B A P X O J L X W Q I O   M
L   T R N D A V Y O D V T S Z M D U   B
I   K K D S N I R M R K A E W N A R   X
R   U M A N I A J X R T L K A M G G   I
E   T U D I A S R A E W U L I K N G   L
L   H L C S G Q P W V F E G G A Q A H
A   J E B Y F F R A N C E T A O Y H V
N   O R W A Y Z S W I T Z E R L A N D
D   W E S T G E R M A N Y K U P B I D
```

From *The Whole Earth Geography Book*, Copyright © 1990 Scott, Foresman and Company.

66

Extended Challenge 11

Match each river in the left column with the names of the
states in the right column that have that river as part of
their border.

A. Colorado River

B. Ohio River

C. Missouri River

D. Columbia River

E. Red River

F. Delaware River

  B   Indiana

  C   Nebraska

  A   California

  E   Oklahoma

  C   Iowa

  B   Ohio

  D   Washington

  F   Pennsylvania

  C   South Dakota

  B   West Virginia

  C   Kansas

  A   Nevada

  E   Arkansas

  F   New Jersey

  D   Oregon

  E   Texas

  B   Illinois

  F   New York

  A   Arizona

  B   Kentucky

Extended Challenge 12

Draw a line from each capital city (left column) to its country
(middle column) and then to that country's continent (right
column). One sample has been done for you.

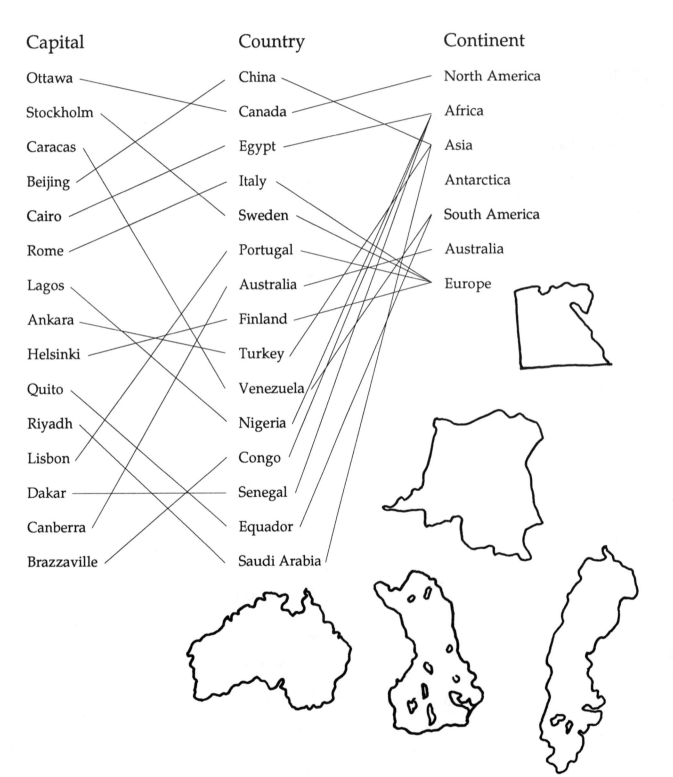

Capital	Country	Continent
Ottawa	China	North America
Stockholm	Canada	Africa
Caracas	Egypt	Asia
Beijing	Italy	Antarctica
Cairo	Sweden	South America
Rome	Portugal	Australia
Lagos	Australia	Europe
Ankara	Finland	
Helsinki	Turkey	
Quito	Venezuela	
Riyadh	Nigeria	
Lisbon	Congo	
Dakar	Senegal	
Canberra	Equador	
Brazzaville	Saudi Arabia	

Extended Challenge 13

Write the state's name in the blank after the clue or description.

1. Mississippi, Georgia, and Alabama are its southern neighbors. _____ Tennessee

2. OK is its state abbreviation. _____ Oklahoma

3. The lowest point in the United States is here. _____ California

4. This state's capital is the same as the name of the sixteenth president. _____ Nebraska

5. This state is mainly a peninsula. _____ Florida

6. The Grand Canyon is located here. _____ Arizona

7. This state has the largest body of salt water within its borders. _____ Utah

8. Frankfort is this state's capital. _____ Kentucky

9. The beginning of the Mississippi River starts here. _____ Minnesota

10. This is the smallest state. _____ Rhode Island

11. Ohio is the eastern neighbor of this state. _____ Indiana

12. Four Great Lakes touch this state. _____ Michigan

13. This state is completely surrounded by water. _____ Hawaii

14. Washington is the northern neighbor of this state. _____ Oregon

15. The Brooks Range is in this state. _____ Alaska

Extended Challenge 14

In the blank, write the name of the country you would be in if you stood at each of the following coordinates.

1. 45°N/0°long _____ France

2. 30°S/31°E _____ South Africa

3. 30°S/150°E _____ Australia

4. 40°N/4°W _____ Spain

5. 45°N/76°W _____ Canada

6. 60°N/75°E _____ USSR

7. 36°N/140°E _____ Japan

8. 30°S/60°W _____ Argentina

9. 15°N/121°E _____ Philippines

10. 45°N/105°E _____ Mongolia

11. 21°N/158°W _____ United States (Hawaii)

12. 15°S/75°W _____ Peru

13. 52°N/0°long _____ England

14. 30°N/30°E _____ Egypt

15. 33°S/71°W _____ Chile

Complete the puzzle below by filling in the spaces with
the names of capitals of Asian countries.

B **A** N G K O K

S E O U L

T **A** I P E I

J **A** K A R T A

R **A** N G O O N

D A **C** C A

U L **A** N   B A T O R

S I N G A **P** O R E

N E W   D E L H **I**

T O K Y O

M A N I L A

C O **L** O M B O

I **S** L A M A B A D